YOUR CAREER IN

REAL ESTATE MANAGEMENT

PROPERTY MANAGER

REAL ESTATE MANAGEMENT IS A FASCINATING CAREER. It requires a great sense of responsibility, patience and understanding of people's needs, a strong footing in finance and property law, and a substantial knowledge of how many things work, from construction equipment, to plumbing and air conditioning, to elevators and ventilation systems. Many people who have chosen this career have done so because of the variety involved and the surprising number of new and unusual challenges that come up on a regular basis. It appeals to people who are too restless to sit in an office all day, but who also appreciate being able to get back to a desk where they can regroup and get themselves organized for the next challenge.

Apparently, the variety plus the high level of activity keeps real estate and property managers happy, as Forbes magazine, in a recent study, ranked this career as second out of the 20 most satisfying jobs in America. Forbes also indicated that these managers have an overall job satisfaction index of 4.7 out of 5.

Besides providing an array of fresh challenges, a career as a real estate manager offers a good salary range and chances for advancement. It is also a career for which substantial growth is seen over the next several years, with estimates of thousands of new real estate and property management jobs becoming available over the course of the next decade.

Under the overall title of real estate manager, there are many additional and more specific titles. The list would include apartment manager, commercial property services coordinator, community manager, condominium association property manager, consulting property manager, lease administration supervisor, leasing manager, on-site property manager, property manager, and resident manager.

Types of properties that a real estate manager might handle include:

- Apartment buildings

- Single-family homes

- Office buildings

- Factories and warehouses

- Shopping centers and other retail locations

- Medical buildings

- Manufactured housing/mobile homes

- Land parcels

Housing comes in several different configurations, including conventionally owned and financed; affordable or public housing (which can be owned by for-profit businesses or nonprofit organizations, or by government agencies); housing specifically for students or seniors; and residential properties that have been converted from straight rentals to condos, co-ops, or are part of a home owners association.

Some real estate management firms work with one or two of these types of properties, while others serve a broad range. Whatever the property type, real estate managers are charged with making sure the properties they are responsible for have an appealing appearance and are well maintained. It is up to them to preserve the property's value, whether for renting, leasing, or resale.

Real estate managers collect the rent, one of the responsibilities that go back to the very origins of the profession. They are often also responsible for advertising and showing available properties to potential new tenants, and dealing with problems between tenants as well as between the tenant and the landlord. It is also their job to evict tenants who either do not pay the rent or who are in violation of rules regarding the use of the property.

It is a job for people with strong personalities who also know how to get along with a wide variety of people. It requires computer skills, the ability to communicate effectively in person and in writing, and a willingness to pitch in and get your hands dirty if the situation calls for it. This would be especially the case when someone is starting out. As an assistant real estate manager, you are more likely to help out the maintenance and janitorial staff when there is a mess that needs cleaning up.

Where can it lead? From an entry-level position, the job can grow into a senior management role. It also serves as a great training ground for getting into real estate sales and even into purchasing or developing your own real estate projects.

THINGS TO DO NOW

IF THE IDEA OF BECOMING A REAL ESTATE MANAGER is appealing to you, then there are several things you can do to begin preparing for this career, starting in your own school. Perhaps the single most important thing you can do is take business classes. As the representative of the property owner whose real estate you are managing, you are also the face of the business. The earlier you can begin to understand how businesses operate, the better your chances of being a capable manager when you land that first job.

Another class that will prove useful in your career as a real estate manager is English, where you will have many writing assignments. Speech classes that require you to get up and speak are a plus. Consider joining the school debate team. As a real estate manager you will likely find yourself in debate mode more often than you might like, with a tenant, a member of the maintenance staff, a product or service vendor, or a member of the community.

Computer skills are a must. Become familiar with accounting programs and record-keeping software, as both will be among the most important tools you will use in this career.

You can also look for opportunities to assist in home building. Look for a local Habitat for Humanity office or any similar organization active in your immediate community. Hands-on experience in construction can be invaluable

More first-hand experience can be gained by visiting a property management office and asking to shadow one of the managers as they go about their work. You can also go out to construction sites (keeping a safe distance, of course), observe how buildings are designed and made. Go often to see the changes as the structure is completed. As much as possible, ask questions of the managers and supervisors present. Learn what products are used in putting the structure together and why. You can also get to know what the janitors and maintenance people at your school do. If you live in an apartment building, get to know your building's support staff.

Pay attention to your surroundings, where you live, where you go to school, where you shop. Try to understand how the buildings around you function, how they are affected by the elements, what could be done to make properties more pleasant, easier to access, more efficient to operate, etc.

Anyone who wants to be in real estate management should learn as much as possible what makes their city/state/community economically strong or what weakens it. You can also investigate local building codes and regulations to see what can and cannot be done when a new structure is being erected. An interesting exercise might be to compare the building codes in your community with those of neighboring communities in order to see what basics are consistently present and what interesting differences might appear.

You can also enhance all of these experiences and activities by reading real estate magazines and professional journals available at no cost online. You can begin to observe trends, find out about the challenges real estate managers have to deal with, and the solutions they come up with.

HISTORY OF REAL ESTATE MANAGEMENT AS A CAREER

IN EARLY HUMAN SETTLEMENTS, individuals were responsible for their own property, although the community as a whole could come together to support someone in need. As the agricultural revolution allowed for larger communities to form, and hierarchies and class structures to develop, ownership of the land and its wealth in many instances went to a single individual ruler such as a king or pharaoh.

These royal personages could not manage so much property on their own. Instead, they came to rely on overseers who could act in their name, making decisions about crops, irrigation, work forces, working conditions, and other critical matters, including building and construction of palaces, pyramids and similar structures. They were the first property managers.

As these hierarchical civilizations gave way to democracies and republics, the role of overseers declined but never disappeared as there continued to be upper classes with more wealth and property than could be managed by the owner alone. The transition of Rome from a republic to an empire brought a great new need for overseers, and the evolution from the Roman Empire to the medieval feudal system continued the need for property managers. A primary element of the work of these professionals was collecting rents from tenants.

The modern era saw a new class of wealthy individuals emerge to replace the nobility as the great powers in European countries. These new lords continued to need the support of professional managers to oversee their properties.

These real estate managers worked directly for the property owners. Throughout the 19th century and into the 20th century in the US and Canada, immigration drove the need for more housing. As the real estate market expanded, there was an ongoing consolidation of ownership. By the 1920s, real estate management began to shift away from working directly for the real estate owners, to a third party management system that could serve many owners at once with a professional, all-encompassing approach.

The stock market crash of 1929 further supported the rise of real estate management as a profession independent of real estate ownership. As many property owners lost their wealth, financial institutions found themselves taking control of the properties for which they held mortgages. Since these banks and other sources of finance had no experience in real estate management they turned to managers to take charge.

The following decades up though the present era have meant an increase in professionalism, in part created by a trend that has seen many real estate management companies choose to specialize in particular types of properties, such as affordable residential housing, commercial buildings, medical facilities, student or senior housing. There has also been an increase in the use of specialized communications equipment as technology has brought a higher level of speed and efficiency to record keeping and financial services.

What was once a profession that was readily open to high school graduates willing to serve an apprenticeship in order to learn the business from the ground up, has now become one that seeks out college graduates and graduates of certification programs offered by training organizations and institutes. In part, this is because of the increased use of technology, but it also reflects a desire to present a more professional face to real estate owners and communal housing associations that are the ones who hire management services.

WHERE YOU WILL WORK

REAL ESTATE MANAGERS TYPICALLY WORK in both an office and onsite at the properties they manage. The job entails a significant amount of administrative work that requires the office setting. Being present at a property is necessary in order to deal with duties such as showing a potential renter around the site, or reviewing repairs or new construction, or meeting with the property owners.

Depending on the size of the management company, the office might accommodate a single person (about 40 percent of property managers are self-employed), but more often there are administrative and support personnel working together, as well as other property managers and executives who oversee the entire operation, even if they are not directly involved with any of the individual properties being managed. Some offices are actually onsite, and the managers are responsible for that particular property rather than managing a portfolio of several units.

The basic types of businesses for which real estate managers work include companies that are strictly devoted to property management, as well as companies that own property that they rent or lease out, and that manage the properties with their own staffs. Real estate managers can also work for firms that do not own the buildings but handle rentals, leasing, and even sales. They might also work for conglomerates that buy and sell properties, offices that handle rentals, or subsidiaries that handle construction, repairs, and services.

Real estate managers who leave the office to go onsite will find themselves visiting a variety of property types including single-family homes, apartment buildings of all sizes, office buildings, factories and warehouses, schools and medical centers, mobile home parks, and even vacant land waiting for some type of construction to begin.

Real estate managers inspect everything in the properties they manage, from basements and boiler rooms, to crawl spaces, to rooftops and all the work and dwelling units. Depending on whether properties are in cities, suburbs, or rural locations, part of the day's work will involve traveling in either public or private transportation.

Because real estate managers need to be close at hand to deal with emergencies, as well as regularly scheduled visits to the properties they manage, there is not much long distance travel involved in this career. Exceptions are when managers are called upon to travel to professional meetings or conventions, or to the home office of their employer if it is a large regional, national, or international management company.

It is worth noting that some apartment managers are required to live in the apartment complexes where they work, so they can be available to respond to emergencies even when they are off duty. In addition, real estate managers often attend meetings with residents, property owners, community association board members, or civic groups that take place in the evening when the participants have finished with their workdays.

THE WORK YOU WILL DO

BEING A REAL ESTATE MANAGER IS A hands-on profession. There will be plenty of work handled at your desk, but also much to be done onsite at the properties for which you will be responsible. It is the type of job where you are as likely to get your hands covered with grease or dirt while helping a janitor deal with a broken pipe, as you are to get a paper cut while loading the office printer.

The office work of real estate managers involves a substantial amount of reading and writing. There are contracts to review, bills to be paid, equipment to be ordered, regulations to be digested, documents to be filed, and reports to be written or studied. In addition, there are phone calls and in-person visits from clients and employers, from current and potential renters and leasers, from contractors and other service providers, and even from government representatives, usually local, who are charged with making sure that buildings and other properties are meeting all regulatory requirements.

Contacts with most of these can be on a regularly scheduled basis to handle routine matters or they may come about to deal with a specific problem or emergency. Tenants and maintenance staff rarely call just to say hello or what a good job the manager is doing. As likely as not, something has gone wrong, either slightly or in a big way, that requires emergency action and you, as the troubleshooter, will have to be on your way.

Some real estate managers indicate that meeting with tenants for one reason or another is something that occurs every single day, almost always onsite. This can include dealing with tenant complaints about the property itself, such as a leaky faucet or peeling paint, disturbances from other tenants, and communication difficulties with the janitorial staff. The manager can also be the one to initiate the contact in order to discuss late payment of rent or complaints against the tenant by neighbors over such issues as pets, parking, or excessive noise. They are also usually in charge of evictions.

Real estate managers typically are responsible for collecting rent money or fees related to the use of the property, or seeing to it that they are paid even if not collecting them personally. They are usually responsible for paying the bills related to the costs of owning and running the property, including such expenditures as taxes, mortgages, insurance, payroll, and maintenance. In addition, they may be responsible for keeping all of the financial statements related to the property, periodically providing reports to the owners on maintenance expenditures, occupancy rates, licenses due for renewal, etc. The real estate manager must deal with the contracts for such services as trash removal, landscaping, security, and other services not provided by the in-house maintenance staff.

At the property, managers may show apartments, office suites, warehouse space, factories, medical facilities, and even vacant lots. When meeting with prospective renters or buyers to show them properties, the real estate manager will typically discuss the lease and explain the terms of occupancy or ownership.

Part of a real estate manager's regular responsibilities is to thoroughly inspect the properties they care for, including building interiors and exteriors, equipment and facility resources, and the grounds and landscaping that are part of the overall property. When they discover a problem, they are responsible for arranging repairs or replacements.

Managers need to keep up-to-date on developments in real estate equipment and services in order to take advantage of any valuable new developments that will improve the lives of tenants and the profitability of the business for their employers, the property owners. A key goal for real estate managers is to ensure that the owners' investments produce maximum revenue gains.

Real estate managers also need to keep up-to-date on changes in the laws and regulations that apply to buildings and land. They need to be ready to comply with any new developments in both federal laws that address discrimination (such as the Americans with Disabilities Act and the Federal Fair Housing Amendment Act), as well as state and local laws that deal with those issues, as well as local building codes and regulations for water, sewer, noise, trash disposal, etc. They should also know safety regulations and be able to instruct both office and maintenance staffs, and tenants, in how to avoid accidents.

Real Estate Agents

Some, but not all real estate managers are engaged in one or more aspects of the selling, buying, and renting or leasing of the properties they manage. In general, this is the work of real estate agents but some managers are agents, either having chosen on their own to obtain a state license or having been required to obtain a license by their employer or by state law.

Real Estate Asset Managers

Some real estate managers are designated as real estate asset managers. They work on behalf of businesses and investors, buying and selling properties but also developing and managing them. These managers, though, do not usually take part in the hands-on, day-to-day operation of the properties, as much as the long-term planning for the property development and potential sale. They are concerned with overall property values, zoning regulations, building codes, and the availability of potential renters. Just as real estate managers have to deal with evictions of tenants, real estate asset managers are concerned with selling properties that are losing value or operating at a loss.

Community Association Management

Some real estate managers specialize in community association management. They work on behalf of residential groups, such as condominiums, time-share and partial ownership, cooperatives, and planned communities, managing the property and services owned by the group as a whole and used jointly by the homeowners in the association.

Community association managers oversee maintenance of the property, handle finances and budgets for building repairs and improvements, collect fees and dues, resolve conflicts among the community members regarding communal rules and regulations, negotiate with contractors, manage the payroll, and make sure that the property and the association are in compliance with all state, local, and federal laws that apply.

Affordable Housing

Real estate managers working in affordable housing or other government supported residential properties will have some specific areas of concern that other managers do not. This involves being familiar with affordable housing and tax credit documentation and the recertification and renewal process, including one-on-one interviews that are required for all residents. It is a real plus when working in affordable housing to have a second and even a third language besides English as many tenants will not be native English speakers.

Commercial and Retail

Real estate managers of commercial and retail properties tend to have a greater degree of familiarity with their tenants than do residential property managers. This is guided by the fact that commercial tenants are usually paying higher rents than residential customers. Residents are usually glad to find a house or apartment that serves their needs and fits their budget. Commercial tenants are more likely to have options regarding where they can operate their businesses and will typically be more demanding than the average apartment resident.

Starting Out

Newcomers to the field will typically gain entry with a job as an assistant real estate or property manager. Some jobs may carry an additional title, such as Maintenance – Facilities Supervisor and emphasize specific areas of concentration, such as handling on-site supervision of facilities maintenance and repairs, working with maintenance workers and subcontractors, and maybe even lending a hand to clean up common areas, changing light bulbs, and making minor property repairs.

It is not unusual for an assistant to be on call and available to deal with emergencies 24/7. The assistant will have the opportunity to deal with the problem first so that hopefully the manager will not have to be called in. Assistant managers often have some staff management opportunities, usually supervising interns or administrative assistants, that gives them another chance to show their employers what they can do.

REAL ESTATE MANAGERS TALK ABOUT THEIR CAREERS

I Grew Up in a Family Where Several Relatives Were Involved in Real Estate

"My dad passed away when I was young, and my mom, brother (who has a degree in Real Estate from the University of Wisconsin), and I became subdivision developers – primarily obtaining entitlements and then the site development. We did both a good sized residential in 3-phases, and an industrial park subdivision. We did some turnkey housing in the last phase.

Even though I was working, I continued with my education, including going to graduate school and earning an MBA (Master of Business Administration degree). I also focused on earning professional credentials, becoming a CPM (Certified Property Manager) and going through a rigorous process to become a CCIM (Certified Commercial Investment Member).

After getting my MBA, I worked for a trust company as an institutional trustee, managing real estate held in trust. It was during this period that I earned my CPM credential that was very useful in the work I was doing then.

I am now executive director of a small nonprofit affordable housing organization. All of my education, training, and experience in managing real estate come into play almost every day. My current position requires experience and expertise in development, successfully applying for grants, navigating the county administration departments, applying for construction loans, understanding and negotiating contracts, bidding construction work, overseeing construction, reporting internally (to the board of directors) and externally to grant providers and lenders, completing housing including punch list items, income qualifying potential homeowners, writing contracts, overseeing escrow through closing, and so much more in between!"

My First Job Was as a Receptionist for a Large Real Estate Management Company

"I completed high school but did not attend college. After working in the office of busy property managers, I asked what I needed to do to get a job like that. The thing that attracted me first, was that I could see there were no two days alike. You don't just sit in a chair all day.

I took my state license sales classes first and then was directed to IREM, the Institute of Real Estate Management, where I studied for and received certification as an ARM (Accredited Residential Manager), and then as a CPM.

I currently oversee a portfolio of 720 units in 11 locations. I work for the owners and monitor a couple of third party management companies that service our portfolio. Some of the things I do each day include property inspections, reviewing financial statements, giving presentations, showing units, meeting with the owners and board of directors, preparing reports, providing resources for support services, taking calls from residents, and also working on capital budgets."

I Manage a Staff of Property Managers and Support Staff

"As a practicing property manager the constant tasks I perform are centered on the physical and financial well-being of the commercial and corporate real estate assets under my care.

I was already out in the work world when I became interested in real estate management, drawn by the diverse nature of the work and responsibilities involved. I have a primary role in such tasks as contracting for lawn and landscape services, janitorial services, building support services such as elevator, fire and life safety equipment, and HVAC equipment.

Providing oversight of those services as well as ensuring that the costs are appropriate is key. Tenant relations, leasing and client relationships are also important functions. Financial tasks such as creating operating and capital budgets, managing those budgets, financial reporting and analysis, and meeting financial objectives of ownership are all key tasks."

I Entered Into Property Management Via Accounting

"As a general ledger accountant for the Building Materials Holding Corporation my duties included balancing the accounts for all the items leased at the 60 locations in the 15 states where BMHC has outlets. I also made sure that the lease payments were sent in a timely manner.

After working for BMHC for three years, I decided to try something else and saw an ad for a small, commercial property management company that needed a property manager. Turned out I knew a lot of the people at the company as they frequented a restaurant that my husband and I owned.

Since I had worked on the tenant side of things, I thought I had the competency to handle the landlord side, and I did. I applied and got the position almost 12 years ago. Most days are spent problem solving in one form or another. Those duties include preparing leases and renewals, fielding calls from tenants and owners, overseeing the billing and collecting of rents for nearly a dozen properties for six owners, paying bills for those properties, and then condensing it all into monthly reports.

To be successful you must be a problem solver. You must be able to look at many sides of a situation and come to a decision that helps the tenants while protecting the property owners' best interests. Having a business degree and experience also helps. Having an understanding of all aspects of building maintenance is also important. You also need the ability and desire to learn and apply new things.

Sometimes I feel like I'm herding cats. Other times I feel like the teacher who patiently, slowly repeats over and over to the owners and tenants things in the lease documents that should be obvious. One example is that a clogged toilet is the tenant's responsibility, but a toilet disconnected from the wax ring or a clogged main sewer line is the owner's responsibility. Other times I feel like a parent. But then there is the other side, the pleasure of helping a business open or expand in one of our commercial spaces."

I Have Been Involved in Property Management Most of My Life

"My father owned rental properties in Alberta, Canada. I enjoyed managing them and learning about real estate investment and other aspects of the business. I wanted to live in Vancouver so I moved there and found a job with a third party national fee-based service property management company. In fact, I'm still with them today and have risen to become the president of the firm. I have also written and designed property management courses and instructed students through the Sauder School of Business, at the University of British Columbia.

My son also works with me. He used to work in the restaurant service business but decided in order to have a family he needed to have more control of his time, and he can do that with property management. We have seven offices across Canada and aside from running the business I work with clients and developers to increase portfolio size. We try to make sure the staff has the latest technology and are educated accordingly.

I like to watch my employees learn as they better themselves professionally and personally, and as they improve and progress in their duties and their careers. I like to see the properties being upgraded, and the clients' appreciation for what we do for them. I like to try new processes and be part of the ever-changing landscape of the profession. It is a good career to choose as many property managers make six figure salaries.

Property management is in its infancy and has a long way to go and will continue to improve as time goes by. People will always need a place to live, our cities are getting larger and densities are getting higher. Real estate needs to be managed and developed efficiently and effectively – they are not making any more of it! It is a career one can practice in any country in the world, the sky is the limit."

I Was Always Interested in Working in the Real Estate Field

"After obtaining my business degree, I worked in real estate sales and investing. I earned my real estate license and dabbled in private property management to get a feel for the real estate management career. A few years later, I attended a workshop from IREM and after listening to a property manager speak about the career, I decided to pursue a career in affordable real estate management for a housing authority.

Currently, I manage affordable housing properties including tax credit, low rent, and senior properties. I have a real estate license and work in sales and private property management, as well. It took approximately seven years to figure out which part of the real estate industry I liked best. There are a lot of different fields to choose from in real estate management, including project development, compliance, managing associations, marketing, etc. I like helping my community with Affordable Tax Credit

Housing and also the possibility of future investments.

I do everything from inspections to budgeting. My duties include explaining different types of affordable housing choices to individuals, explaining eligibility and application screening processes, running background checks, verifying applicant data, entering data in property management software, scheduling leasing appointments and unit showings, creating lease documents, processing move ins and move outs, overseeing property house rules and managing complaints and violations, collecting rents, assessing necessary fees, posting notices, creating work orders, assisting with improvement plans, overseeing units to be turned over for new residents, comparing rental pricing and comps, and advertising and managing contractors.

Interpersonal communication is extremely important in this business. Also, being a trainer or teacher helps. Many renters don't understand the reason behind the policies and know very little about fair housing laws. Marketing is a great skill as well.

I enjoy helping housing residents who are working hard to improve themselves, and housing residents who need assistance and have had trouble finding a place of their own. Additionally, I enjoy keeping the rentals in good condition and being proud of the units I rent, and the properties I oversee. I want people to love their home, and be proud of it as well.

I think there will always be opportunities in the real estate field. I believe education and training in property management are greatly needed so managers understand the laws which protect tenants and landlords, and the processes which are appropriate to use in the real estate management field."

I Started My Career in Maintenance and Facilities Management

"I became interested in work my bosses were doing at the time, so I took some classes and started my career in property management.

Some of my specific duties include budgeting, accounting and delinquency management, managing construction projects, handling leases and customer service. The single greatest challenge in this job is handling difficult people.

Statistics show that there will be a shortage of property managers entering the field. The average age of property managers in the field now is around 50 years old. As these individuals retire there will be an abundance of jobs in the property management field. Property management is resilient and recession-resistant as people always need a place to live."

PERSONAL QUALIFICATIONS

REAL ESTATE MANAGEMENT IS A CUSTOMER SERVICE CAREER, requiring strong interpersonal skills, as you will be dealing on a daily basis with property owners, renters, service providers, and government officials, each of whom expects you to give them your full attention. You must be able to listen to, absorb, and respond appropriately to their problems, concerns, and needs.

Occasionally you might also hear some praise and will want to express your appreciation. More often than not, however, you will be hearing about problems that need fixing. An even temperament and the ability to keep your cool when other people are in a rage or on their way to one are critical.

This is also a career that requires solid organizational skills. Most real estate managers deal with a portfolio of properties and as a result face a multitude of situations that require many different solutions. You will have to determine which problem solver needs to be connected to which problem, with what resources, and in what time frame. Some people have an instinct for this kind of decision-making, but it is also something that can be learned.

Real estate managers need to have basic business skills, especially when it comes to financial matters. A knowledge of economic and accounting principles and practices is fundamental. Having good math skills come to the fore in this arena. In addition, an awareness of real estate market trends, especially in the communities where your properties are located, is extremely valuable. Similarly, knowledge of local real estate laws and regulations related to occupancy, construction, transportation, health, safety, and environmental issues are critical.

Your career in real estate management can be enhanced by your familiarity and experience with construction equipment, supplies, and methods. This can help you gauge the cost and time of repair projects so that the information you pass on to owners and tenants is not simply what the service provider told you.

Even though as a real estate manager you are not usually involved directly in sales, it is helpful that you understand sales and marketing issues and techniques. Sales personnel and rental agents may call upon you for support or to explain details about the property to potential buyers or renters. Helping to close a deal is always a good thing.

ATTRACTIVE FEATURES

REAL ESTATE MANAGERS ARE OFTEN DRAWN to this career because of the variety of activities in which they get to participate. It is a great opportunity for people who like a mix of office work and onsite activity; who enjoy getting out and talking to tenants, as well as being focused on selecting just the right word for the report they are preparing; and who are just as comfortable at a meeting in a corporate boardroom as they are inspecting insulation in a crawlspace.

Part of the appeal of the variety in this career is that so much of it happens in a single day, going back and forth between your   office and different properties, meeting with tenants, maintenance staff, construction foremen, government representatives, and the property owners. Then it is back to the office to update the records on all the activities in which you engaged.

It is a great career for a problem solver, as many, if not most, of the visits to the properties and the meetings that take place are because something has gone wrong or there is some other reason for complaint. It also is great for someone who can make decisions quickly and decisively.

The work of a real estate manager is demanding, without question, but it has rewards. In term of earnings, the median is about $55,000 with the potential to become a six-figure salary as one accumulates experience.

Many real estate managers, especially those who work in some form of affordable or public housing, report the emotional reward they get when they have the opportunity to help people in need. This can take the form of helping families find decent shelter, or providing them with guidance and support while they are settling into a new environment.

Real estate managers also have the opportunity to serve their employers by finding ways to improve the properties for which they are responsible. There are always some areas in which properties can be upgraded. For people who take pride in their work, there will be opportunities to shine.

UNATTRACTIVE FEATURES

DESPITE THE MANY APPEALING features of a career as a real estate manager, it can be very stressful work. Even if you enjoy being a problem solver, there can be times when there are too many problems that all need to be solved immediately. Finding enough time to get everything done is, according to some real estate managers, the biggest challenge in their work. They feel they could do more, could do better, if only time permitted.

The stress levels can affect everyone involved, so that the tension you may be feeling can also affect the people you are dealing with. People who are usually great to get along with can be less than pleasant when the pressure is on. This can include tenants, staff, government officials, contractors, and the property owners.

There will be times when a difficult situation cannot be avoided, particularly when someone needs to be evicted. Most real estate managers agree that evicting a tenant, especially if it is a family, from their home, whether an apartment or a house, is the hardest and most distressing part of the job. Sometimes just trying to get tenants to follow the provisions of their leases, such as not playing music after a certain hour or not leaving a bicycle in a foyer, can make for an awful day's work.

Depending on the organization you work for, there can be situations when there is not enough money available to make repairs properly or in a timely fashion. Sometimes the owners do not have the money needed and sometimes they simply do not want to spend it. In either case, it is up to the real estate manager to find a workaround.

The real estate manager can be the person responsible for dealing with government red tape, something especially convoluted when it comes to housing, construction, and building codes. The simplest request for an improvement in a building's plumbing can involve dealing with the water department, the housing department, sanitation, etc.

EDUCATION AND TRAINING

A COLLEGE DEGREE IS NOT ESSENTIAL for getting started in real estate management. You may be able to land an entry-level position and get on-the-job training that will allow you to advance in this career. Experience in any other type of management position and in real estate sales are also valuable.

It is a better idea to get a college degree even if you obtain it after you have already started working in this field. The degrees that are most applicable to success in real estate management include a bachelor's or master's degree in real estate, or in business administration, accounting, finance, or public administration.

The Institute for Real Estate Management points out that "since the mid-1980s there has been a steady increase in real estate degree programs within colleges and universities throughout the US. Once known as a profession learned on the job, real estate has now become a field that demands further education. For those entering in the field of real estate or property management or considering a graduate degree to leverage career advancement, earning a degree in real estate may be the answer. Many colleges and universities offer real estate or property management degrees, at undergraduate and graduate levels."

Participating in a degree program can have the added benefit of providing direct contact with industry professionals. Students in the residential property management program at Ball State, for example, interact with property management and apartment industry professionals "through class projects, field trips, internships, conferences, and professional networking events." These industry professionals serve as class speakers and also make guest appearances at meetings for the student organization,

Residential Property Management Association (RPMA).

Among the schools mentioned by the Institute of Real Estate Management (IREM) as offering degrees specifically in property management are:

- University of Alaska – Anchorage
- University of Georgia
- Ball State University – Indiana
- Curry College – Massachusetts
- Dakota County Technical College
- Saint Augustine's University
- Drexel University
- University of North Texas
- University of Texas – San Antonio
- Brigham Young University
- Virginia Polytechnic University
- University of Wisconsin – Stout

In Canada, the University of British Columbia and the University of Guelph offer BA degrees in Real Estate and Housing. In addition, Humber College in Toronto, in cooperation with the Institute of Housing Management (IHM), presents a certificate program in the management and operations of publicly and privately owned residential and institutional buildings.

There are additional schools offering online certification programs in real estate management.

Undergraduate Degrees

Undergraduate degrees related to real estate and property management include four-year degrees such as Bachelor of Arts, Bachelor of Science, Bachelor of Business Administration, and Bachelor of Science in Business Administration. Two-year degrees include Associate of Arts, Associate of Applied Science, and Associate of Science. Some schools offer certificate programs as well as degree programs.

A sampling of the classes offered in undergraduate real estate management programs around the country includes:

- Affordable Housing Management

- Apartment Financial Management

- Building Codes

- Building Systems for Property Management

- Commercial Property Appraisal

- Commercial Property Financial Reporting

- Computer Applications for Property Management Professionals

- Customer Relations

- Customer Service Theory/Practice

- Health Services and the Elderly

- Hospitality Facilities Management

- Housing & Society

- Housing Decisions

- Housing for Seniors

- Human Resources for Property Managers

- Introduction to Property Management

- Introduction to Real Estate

- Introduction to Residential Property Management

- Issues in Aging and Longevity

- Legal Aspects of Real Estate

- Maintenance for Property Managers

- Management of Government-Assisted Housing

- Managing and Marketing Housing for an Aging Population

- Managing and Marketing Industrial Properties

- Managing and Marketing Office Buildings

- Managing and Marketing Retail Property

- Marketing and Leasing Residential Property

- Military Housing Management

- Principles of Accounting

- Principles of Design

- Principles of Marketing

- Property Financing & Valuation

- Property Management Technology

- Property Risk Management

- Race and Ethnic Relations

- Real Estate Facilities & Property Management

- Rental Property and Fair Housing Law

- Residential Technologies

- Social Responsibility for Property Managers

- Sociology of the Aging

- Student Housing Management

- Sustainable Property Management

- Technical Drawings for Property Managers

- Urban Sociology

Graduate Degrees

Several of the schools offer graduate degrees related to real estate, including Master of Business Administration, Master of Professional Studies, Master of Real Estate, Master of Real Estate Development, and Master of Science in Real Estate. While the programs touch on real estate and property management, their main focus is on development and marketing.

The graduate programs at Ball State University in Indiana, Northwestern University in Illinois, Ohio State University, and Drexel University appear to focus more on management. Ball State features an master's degree with emphasis in residential property management. Northwestern has a master's with a real estate management major; Ohio State, a degree with a real estate management career track; and Drexel, a graduate degree in property management, offered online for people already working in the career.

Licenses, Certifications, and Credentials

There are only a few regulations that apply to real estate managers. There are a handful of states that require property and community association managers to have a real estate license. In addition, a federal regulation requires that property managers of public housing subsidized by the federal government must hold certifications.

Property managers working in Alaska, Colorado, California, Connecticut, Florida, Georgia, Illinois, Nevada, Virginia, and the District of Columbia are required to obtain professional credentials or licensure and renew them periodically.

There are several organizations that provide classes and training that lead to professional certifications and credentials. These include BOMI International, Certified Commercial Investment Member Institute, Community Association Managers International Certification Board, Community Associations Institute, Institute of Real Estate Management, the National Association of Residential Property Managers, and the Real Estate Institute of Canada.

EARNINGS

THE MEDIAN ANNUAL WAGE FOR PROPERTY, real estate, and community association managers is about $60,000. The median wage is the figure at which half the workers in an occupation earn more than that amount and half earn less. In the case of real estate managers, the lowest 10 percent earn about $30,000, and the highest 10 percent earn more than $120,000.

Median annual salaries for these managers in the top industries in which they work are estimated as follows:

- Offices of real estate agents and brokers $55,000

- Civic, social, professional, and similar organizations $53,000

States reporting the highest annual earnings are New York, Maryland, Texas, Massachusetts, and Virginia. The figures range from about $110,000 in New York, down to about $86,000 in Virginia. The top metro areas are New York State's Nassau/Suffolk Counties; San Francisco; Dallas; Bakersfield, California; New York/New Jersey; Baltimore; Richmond, Virginia; Boston; Syracuse, New York; and Houston.

OUTLOOK

EMPLOYMENT OF PROPERTY, REAL ESTATE, and community association managers in the US is projected to grow by about eight percent within the coming decade, slightly faster than the average for all occupations. Forecasts have the category growing by over 25,000 jobs from its current level of about 315,000, to reach almost 340,000.

As the field becomes more competitive, the best chances for landing a job will belong to those who hold a college degree in business administration or real estate, as well as for those who go on to obtain professional credentials. Most jobs will be full time, although currently about one in five real estate managers works part time.

Growth will be driven by the increase in new dwellings, both multi-unit housing – whether public or private, rentals, condos, or coops – and from single homes that are in planned communities managed by homeowner associations that provide professionally managed services to members. In addition, owners of existing properties that have managed them in-house, will increasingly look to external management services, recognizing the value these services contribute to improving the resale prices of homes and commercial property.

Opportunities will also be created by a wave of retirements by baby boomers. Retirements in the general population will also factor into the equation as a projected increase in the elderly population will drive the need for real estate managers for retirement centers, age-restricted communities, and healthcare facilities.

Industry participants are optimistic that the field will continue to grow in the coming years. There appears to be a general agreement that people with the right skills and work ethic will always be able to find work as real estate managers.

States with the highest levels of real estate management jobs are California, Texas, Illinois, New York, and Florida. Metro regions with high employment levels are Los Angeles, New York, Chicago, Atlanta, Phoenix, Houston, Miami, District of Columbia, and Minneapolis/St. Paul.

GETTING STARTED

IN YEARS PAST, A HIGH SCHOOL GRADUATE could find an opening with a real estate management company and learn the trade through what amounted to an apprenticeship. In the current employment market, real estate management professionals stress the importance of getting both a college degree and certification from one of the recognized institutions that confer such recognition and credentials. In addition, current professionals strongly suggest that the more education one has – in communications, project management, advertising, mathematics, real estate law, ethics and general real estate – the better.

Real estate managers usually recommend that when you are ready to start out, you should join the Institute of Real Estate Management (IREM) or another real estate management association and take the classes that they offer. Membership in these organizations also offers great networking events where you can meet professionals in the field and obtain leads into the industry.

While degrees and credentials are certainly of top value, it is not to say that there are no opportunities available while you are going to school or going through the certification process. Real estate managers encourage young people to seek out management companies to see if they are willing to accept interns. They note that any experience is important if it helps get your foot in the door, and you can get a head start on your job hunting through hands-on, on-site experience.

In addition, professionals in the field encourage young people starting out to find a good mentor, someone who can serve as a one-to-one guide through the ins and outs of being a real estate manager. If there is no single person who can serve you in this capacity, look to build relationships with a network of people in this field. In fact, a network could have more value if the individuals are engaged in different areas of the process of managing a property. You should aim to learn about how things work, not just physically but operationally. Do not inhibit your own curiosity. Learn about furnaces, economic cycles, and demographics.

Most of all, learn the day-to-day tasks and activities that are part of the basic process of going from the first advertising of the availability of a property, to preparing a unit of occupancy, all the way to when someone moves out of a space and the process starts again.

ORGANIZATIONS

■ **AIR Commercial Real Estate Association**
www.airea.com

■ **American Apartment Owners Association**
www.american-apartment-owners-association.org

■ **American Association of Small Property Owners**
http://aaspo.org

■ **American Escrow Association**
www.a-e-a.org

■ **APPA: Leadership in Educational Facilities**
http://www.appa.org

■ **BOMI International**
www.bomi.org

■ **Canadian Real Estate Association**
www.crea.ca

■ **Certified Commercial Investment Member Institute**
www.ccim.com

■ **Community Associations Institute**
www.caionline.org

■ **Community Association Managers International Certification Board**
www.camicb.org

■ **International Facilities Management Association**
www.ifma.org

■ **Institute of Housing Management**
https://ihmcanada.net

■ Institute of Real Estate Management
www.irem.org

■ NAIOP, The Commercial Real Estate Development
Association
www.naiop.org

■ National Apartment Association
www.naahq.org

■ National Association of Real Estate Investment
Managers
www.nareim.org

■ National Association of Residential Property Managers
www.narpm.org

■ National Multifamily Housing Council
www.landlord.com

■ National Association of Realtors
www.realtor.org

■ Network of Commercial Real Estate Women
www.crewnetwork.org

■ Onsite Property Management Association
http://theopma.org

■ Property Management Association
www.pma-dc.org

■ Real Estate Institute of Canada
www.reic.ca

■ Real Estate Research Institute
www.reri.org

www.ingramcontent.com/pod-product-compliance
Lightning Source LLC
Chambersburg PA
CBHW061236180526
45170CB00003B/1326